9 INNINGS WITH

CAL RIPKEN JR

BY THE PEOPLE WHO KNOW HIM BEST

EARL WEAVER • ALEX RODRIGUEZ • CAL'S PARENTS
BRADY ANDERSON • JON MILLER • HAROLD REYNOLDS

9 INNINGS WITH CAL RIPKEN JR.

Copyright©1998 by Dr. James Beckett

All rights reserved under International and Pan-American Copyright Conventions.

9 Innings with Cal is not licensed, authorized or endorsed by any league, player or players association, nor is it authorized or endorsed by Cal Ripken Jr.

Published by: Beckett Publications, 15850 Dallas Parkway, Dallas, TX 75248

Manufactured in the United States of America

ISBN: 1-887432-46-9

Cover photo by Gregory Heisler / Outline

First Edition: November 1998

The Rock

In the following first-person essays on Cal Ripken Jr., major league players and managers — even Cal's father — say they hope the Iron Man's consecutive games played record doesn't overshadow his Hall of Fame-caliber feats as a deft-fielding, power-hitting shortstop and leader of the Baltimore Orioles.

At the same time, they know what people will think of first when they hear the name Cal Ripken Jr. Tomorrow. A year from now. Ten years from now. They'll think of The Streak, and many will remember The Night in Baltimore when Cal broke the games played mark of Lou Gehrig.

"Incomprehensible," Paul Molitor says of The Streak. If Cal's mark boggles the mind of a member of the 3,000-hit club, what are we supposed to think? One thing is for sure. People won't give a first thought to the freak injuries that sidelined other big-leaguers during Cal's run of perfect attendance.

Here are just a few mishaps compiled by Jim Caple, who covers the majors for the *St. Paul* (Minn.) *Pioneer Press.* All prove why The Streak defies logic, and all support Molitor's widely held stance that Jr. "is the rock of the game."

• Rickey Henderson missed several games due to frostbite — in August.

• Vince Coleman missed the 1985 World Series when he got rolled up in the tarp machine.

• Rick Aguilera missed two months when he injured his wrist lifting his wife's suitcase.

• Kevin Mitchell suffered a strained muscle while vomiting.

• Pitcher Steve Foster suffered a shoulder injury after knocking over milk bottles during a segment with Jay Leno on *The Tonight Show.*

• Wade Boggs missed several games after straining his back while pulling on his cowboy boots.

• Milwaukee's Dave Nilsson missed the early part of the '95 season with Ross River Fever, a mosquito-borne virus that annually affects 200 of Australia's 17 million citizens.

• Outfielder Bret Barberie missed a game after he rubbed habanero chili juice in his eye.

• Doc Gooden missed a start when Vince Coleman accidentally hit him with a golf club.

• Pitcher Steve Sparks dislocated his shoulder while tearing a phone book in half.

• Chris Brown missed a game after he strained an eyelid by sleeping on his eye funny.

• In what must be considered the quintessential modern athletic injury, Tony Gwynn missed a couple of games after he smashed his thumb in the door of his luxury car — while going to the bank.

CONTENTS

"Cal's streak doesn't say so much about the ability of the man as it does about the character of the man. I think he is the rock of the game." — Paul Molitor, longtime opponent and admirer

BY CAL RIPKEN SR.

HENRY LOUIS GEHRIG
JUNE 19TH 1903 — JUNE 2ND 1941

A MAN, A GENTLEMAN
AND
A GREAT BALL PLAYER
WHOSE AMAZING RECORD
OF 2130 CONSECUTIVE GAMES
SHOULD STAND FOR ALL TIME

THIS MEMORIAL IS A TRIBUTE
FROM THE PLAYERS

That was without a doubt a marvelous day (when Cal Ripken Jr. broke Lou Gehrig's consecutive games played record). It was a marvelous few days, an unbelievable few days. I had been watching the games on TV leading up to it. I hadn't been down to the stadium. I would sit there, and when the fifth inning came around (in the games leading up to the night he broke the record) with the standing ovation and he would reply to the crowd, I would think, "Let the guy wave and play shortstop. The first guy might pull it down there and he might have to make a play."

But being in the stadium . . . there are no words to describe how that stadium was. I remember I leaned over to a gal sitting next to me and said, "Being in this ballpark at this time makes the World Series seem like an exhibition game." You couldn't believe how it was.

I remember a lot of little things about that night. I remember him running around the stadium, and how the crowd wouldn't stop cheering. Cal had said, "I don't want the game to be delayed a long time."

Raffy (Rafael Palmeiro) and (Bobby) Bonilla pushed him out there. One thing led to another and he didn't have any choice. When he started around the park . . . it was unbelievable. I have never seen anything like that.

What happened that night and how he handled it was incredible. I marvel at the way he handles everything. All the attention he gets is part of the game and he understands that. He has the ability to understand things and figure out what's going to take place before it happens. He understands those things have to be handled the same way as going out and fielding a ground ball. There's a right way to go about it and there's a wrong way to go about it.

He knew about this because he had the oppor-

Sept. 6, 1995, was the day baseball, and all of sports, stood still. After five innings, when the Orioles' game against the California Angels had become official, Cal Ripken Jr. celebrated breaking Lou Gehrig's record of consecutive games played with a victory lap around Oriole Park at Camden Yards.

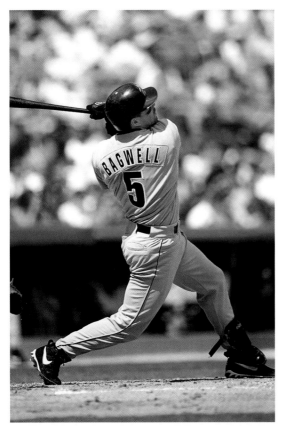

tunity of being around the ballpark, of seeing writers come in the clubhouse and interview players. He had opportunity to see writers interview me. When he came to the ballpark as a young kid, he saw how things were done before the game and how they were handled after the game. He paid attention to everything and stored that in his memory bank.

I think that helped him. He had an idea of how it should be done, and he made a decision how he wanted to play the game and how he wanted to handle the media and how he wanted to handle the pressures with everything that goes with the game.

His daily exposure to the game, I think, also helped him in setting the record. The Streak came about, as Cal always said, by playing a 162-game season, and after all these seasons, it winds up to where he's at now. Even with some of my youth soccer clubs, Cal was a kid who came to the field to play. From my side of the fence, as a manager or coach, you want players that want to play. You don't want people who come to the park and don't want to play.

By going out and playing every day, The Streak evolved. That's the only way you can look at it. He didn't start out to do that. He had no intention of that. The only thing he wanted to do was play 162 games a year, take a few months off, then do it again.

There were times when he was injured, but I don't think he ever thought about it ending. He was always thinking about the next day's game. You don't think beyond that. I remember Earl (Weaver) was managing the club when we had an exhibition game against the Naval Academy. Cal didn't play

After the 1997 season, Houston's Craig Biggio was second among active players in consecutive games played and needed 2,097 straight games to catch Ripken. Teammate Jeff Bagwell, third, needed 2,126. Of course, Ripken hasn't exactly stopped adding to his total of 2,478 consecutive games through the 1997 season.

In addition to his father, Ripken has played under six Orioles managers. In order, they are (top row, left to right): Earl Weaver (1981-82, 1985-86), Joe Altobelli (1983-85), (second row) Frank Robinson (1988-91), Johnny Oates (1991-94), (third row) Phil Regan (1995) and Davey Johnson (1996-97).

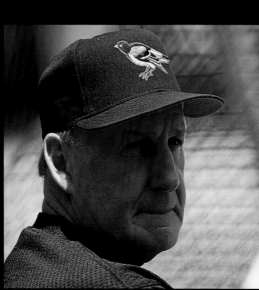

because of a sprained ankle, but the next day he played.

I really think had we been playing a league game that day, he would have been ready to play. But, it was an exhibition game and Earl and the trainers thought there was no point in playing him when he could have a day off.

There's an old theory in the game of baseball that says, "Let's take care of today, then we'll look at tomorrow." That's the nature of the business, to play them one game at a time. When the press is interviewing the manager, he says, "We'll take them one day at a time." That's the first state-ment that comes out. You can't play tomorrow's game until you play today's game. That's how Cal has always handled it, and I think that's the only way he could approach The Streak.

What also helped is he loves the game of base-ball. I have always been a firm believer that you should go out and do what you enjoy doing. There are too many people in the world who have to work at jobs they don't enjoy doing — and Cal loves baseball.

Cal always loved the game, but he also knew how difficult it would be to reach this level. When he was with me when I was managing in the minor leagues, he was aware of how difficult things could

On Aug. 17, 1933, Yankees first baseman Lou Gehrig played in his 1,308th straight game to break the major league record held by former Yankee teammate Everett Scott. The Iron Horse eventually played in 2,130 straight games before the effects of amy-otrophic lateral sclerosis (better known as Lou Gehrig's disease) ended the streak.

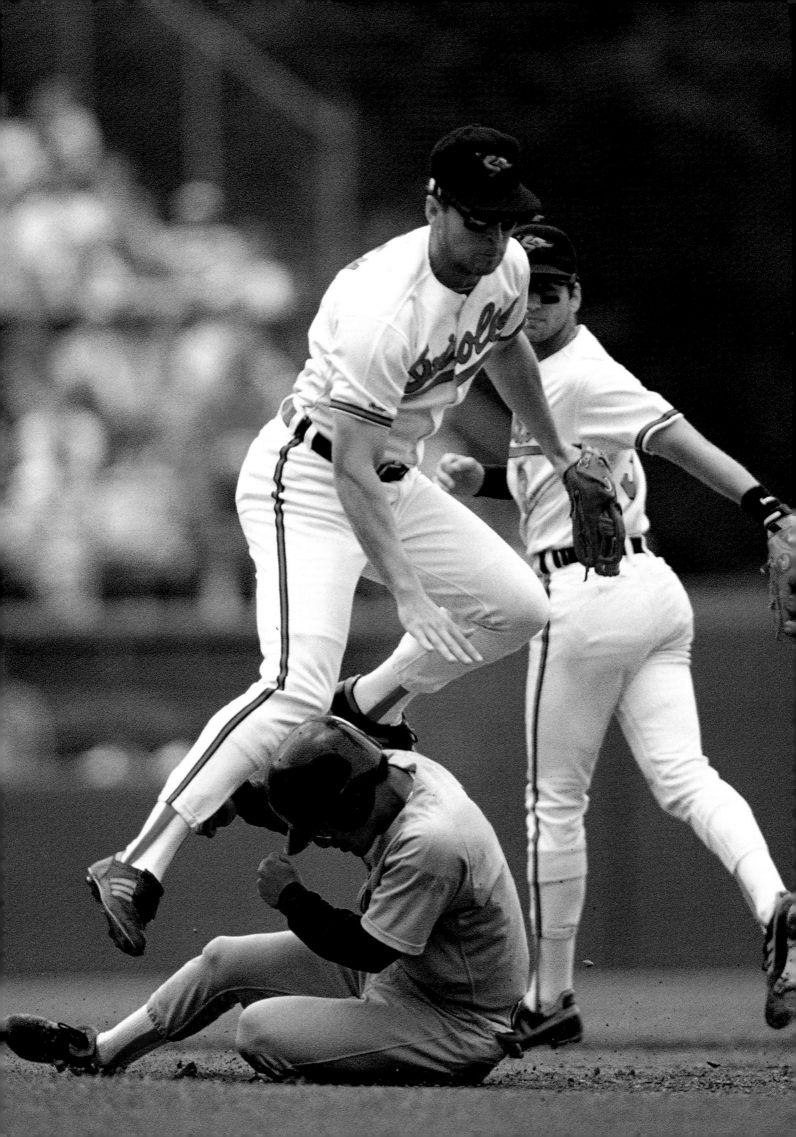

You won't hear Cal complaining about off-season workouts. At his home gym, Ripken can be found lifting weights, swinging bats and running laps. His home basketball court is complete with an electronic scoreboard.

get in the minor leagues and how difficult it was to get to the big leagues. I encouraged him, yes, because that's what he wanted to do, but he always knew how hard he would have to work to reach that level.

Cal always had ability, but nobody is smart enough to know watching him in high school that he was going to make it to the major leagues. There's nobody that smart in the world. You can

look at a guy's physical tools — his abilities to catch a ball, throw a ball, hit a ball and hit a ball with power and run — and you can project. Managing in the minor leagues for 14 years, I saw a lot of guys come through with all the ability in the world, but they didn't make it to the big leagues because they lacked other things.

Nobody was smart enough to know when Cal Jr. was in high school that he would make the big

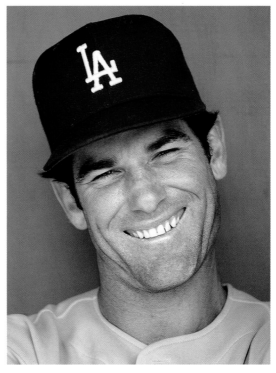

Without the fanfare of the 2,131 night in Baltimore, Sachio Kinugasa's international record of 2,216 straight games fell quietly with a handshake in Kansas City. Former Dodger Steve Garvey, who played in 1,207 straight games for the Dodgers and Padres, holds the National League consecutive games played record.

leagues. The scouts who saw him play in high school saw him play well and saw him do the things that made them think, "This kid has some ability." But nobody could project he would go on and do all that he's accomplished.

With my background, I didn't start to think about professional baseball for Cal until he was a junior in high school. I had the opportunity to see him work out at Memorial Stadium and the things I saw indicated he had the ability to play professionally.

One thing I saw was his desire to work hard. I was honored to hear the things he said about me that night. He has a strong work ethic, and it's a possibility he picked that up from me because he saw the way I went about things and worked at things. I know he's heard me say to the minor league players that you have to work hard to get to the big leagues, and when you get to the big leagues

Of Cal Ripken Jr., teammate Mike Mussina says, "He's going to play until he stops breathing. We're going to wheel him out there in a wheelchair, he'll move himself into position, be right there when the ball comes and throw the runner out at first."

you have to work hard to stay there.

You have to work hard to be good at anything. You have to apply yourself. There's only one way to do things and that's to do it the right way. It doesn't take any longer to do it the right way. You do it the right way, and that's the only way I know how to go about it.

The game of baseball is a repetitious game. You practice in order to play the game the same way. This is why you have to form the good habits on the sidelines, with anything prior to the game being the sidelines. This is where you form the good habits that carry over into the game. Cal has done that, and those habits are what made The Streak possible.

In some ways, it is a little unfair because The Streak may have detracted from some of the other things he has done. If you go back and look at his record in the major leagues, he's had consistent years from the time he started until now.

Then you build a ballclub you look for consistency. Let's take Eddie Murray. You look at Eddie Murray and know he's going to hit you 30 home runs and drive in 100 runs. You'll see the same thing applies with Cal. You know he's going to drive in 90 runs, you know he's going to play good defense, you know he's going to hit 20 home runs. The Streak detracts a little bit from what he has done each year and the value he has been to a ballclub. He's put up some very good numbers over the years.

Cal Ripken is a baseball legend, says teammate Brady Anderson. Still, when he signs autographs he adds a "Jr." tail as a tribute to his father, Cal Ripken Sr.,

who spent more than 30 years with the Baltimore Orioles as a player, third base coach and manager.

In 1987, Ripken Sr. became the first father to manage two sons — Cal and Billy — simultaneously. On August 25, 1996, Cal Ripken Sr. was inducted into the Baltimore Orioles Hall of Fame.

On the night of Sept. 6, 1995, Ripken Sr. watched his son step into baseball history and cap a 22-minute standing ovation with a memorable lap around the outfield at Camden Yards. It was also the night the normally reserved son publicly thanked his father.

"He inspired me with his commitment to the Oriole tradition and made me understand the importance of it," Ripken said. "He not only taught me the fundamentals of the game of baseball, but he also taught me to play it the right way, and to play it the Oriole way. From the beginning, my dad let me know how important it was to be there for your team and to be counted on by your teammates."

John Delcos covers the Orioles for The York (Penn.) Daily Record.

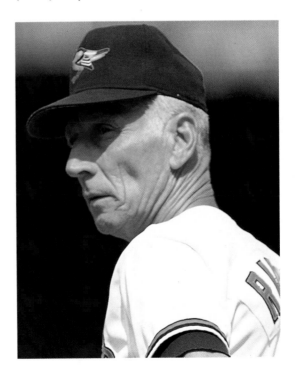

BY JOHNNY OATES

A lot of people would like to be leaders. They want to be leaders. But I don't think the most vocal guy is always the best leader.

A leader is a guy who earns the respect of his teammates because of the way he plays the game. There are great players who can't lead, and there are fringe players who are great leaders. The best term I have is that they have a "presence" about them.

The guys I've been associated with in the clubhouse who were, in my mind, leaders are Cal Jr., Mickey Tettleton, Will Clark, Mike Henneman, Rick Sutcliffe, Bob Tewksbury. Their teammates respected them, because they knew they could be counted on in tough situations. They were team first, and the individual came second. They were winners and they were guys who had the respect of their teammates.

You can't teach that. Cal Jr.'s the same way.

You can't teach it; it's an acquired taste. I don't know if leaders are born, but it certainly takes more than to say, "I'm going to be a leader."

If it was easy to be a leader, there would be more of them. And there are more followers in this game than there are leaders.

I didn't know Cal very much as a younger player. He and I played catch when he was 6 years old. It was winter Instructional League, and

Johnny Oates (left) played for Cal Ripken Sr. in the Class A Florida State League in 1967 and credits Ripken Sr. for helping him develop his skills as a player and a leader. Oates later watched Cal Jr. pass on much of the same knowledge to teammates.

his dad (Cal Sr.) was the manager. I'd come early to the ballpark, and he'd be there, wanting to play catch at 8 o'clock in the morning.

I didn't really run into Cal again until I was released by the Yankees in 1981 and went to (Triple-A) Columbus as a player/coach. He played third base for Rochester (N.Y.), and I saw him a little bit in the International League that year. And then I really didn't see him again until 1989, when I joined the Orioles' staff. So I really didn't know Junior as a young player.

But, knowing how analytical he was — and his dad — I'd think he's always been that way. Always thinking things out. Knowing what's supposed to be done. It's nothing you can teach. You just sit down and it comes to you. You can teach some of it, but you can't teach all of it. Some of it was just the innate knowledge of what needs to be done.

It was like Senior used to teach us. People talk about practice, practice, practice, and he'd say, "That's wrong. It's perfect practice." You can practice and practice it wrong, and what good does it do you? The idea is to practice it right. You see that in Junior, and that perfect practice wears off on other players. Taking infield. Taking batting practice. Playing the game. Being in the right spot.

Junior was one of those players who knew what everybody else on the field was supposed to be doing. And it bothered him, even in spring training, to do cutoffs and relays (drills) with the first group not there. He wanted it done right. He didn't want one guy in the minor league camp doing cutoffs and relays with the big-league team, because he messed it up. He wanted everybody to see, "This is the way it's supposed to be done." We weren't doing cutoffs and relays for three or four guys, we were doing it for the whole team, including those kids waiting their turns on the sidelines.

Do it right. That's what made him a leader. Practice it right. There is a right way to do things, and if it wasn't worth doing right, it wasn't worth doing.

Oates says Cal only knows one way to hit, field or do anything else in life, and that's the right way.

"I always knew Cal was a good player," says teammate Rafael Palmeiro. "But I never knew how great a player he is until I got the chance to play with him day after day. If you saw him play once or twice, he might not amaze you, but if you see him day after day, you appreciate all the little things he does to help his team win."

In 1992, Cal won the Roberto Clemente Award, given to the player who best exemplifies the game of baseball both on and off the field. That same year, he also won the Lou Gehrig Award, given by the Phi Delta Theta national collegiate fraternity to the major leaguer who best fits the image and character of the Hall of Fame first baseman.

Cal Jr. was a guy who, when you went to organize spring training, you made sure that it was organized in the proper way. In other words, if you had a group of players who had to go to Fields 1, 2 and 3 — in that order — you made sure they didn't have to go to 1, 3 and 2. Because Cal would come up and say, "Well, why don't we stop off at 2 on the way to 3? It would save time, and we would get a lot more work done." That's the way it was going to be, because he was very analytical.

He was very analytical about work, very analytical about the game. He never wanted to miss infield (drills) because he said it was the closest thing he'd have to game situations before the game.

Very competitive. It doesn't matter if it was marbles. As a kid, he busted his head open when he

Oates now faces the tough task of coaching against Cal, who has flirted with the .300 mark as a hitter against Texas throughout his amazing career.

set his sister up for a triple jump in checkers, and she fell for it. He did it and jumped up and hit his head on some cabinet or something, and they put 15 stitches in or something like that. I don't know the whole story, but that's the worst injury he ever had. He's just a competitive guy.

I don't know how he plays every day. Physically, I see how he does it. But mentally, I don't know. I think that's the strongest thing about Cal, how tough he is mentally. Cal is not a guy, I think, who will go out of his way to share his thoughts and feelings. But if you sat him down

and started talking to him, he was really fun to talk to.

Sometimes, he got so deep you'd get tired of thinking, "What's this guy really trying to tell me?" But I'm thankful that I had the opportunity to be associated not only with him, but with his dad and with the entire family. Because 98 percent of the stuff I believe in today is what Cal Sr. taught me in 1967, 30 years ago, my rookie year.

I can say stuff now, even here in Texas, and Billy (Ripken) will say, "You got that from my dad, didn't you?" Stuff like, during batting practice, no one's allowed to run the bases carrying a bat. After making an out, you don't throw your batting helmet, you hand it to a coach. Personally, I thought it was a pretty good idea when he told me, "Don't throw your helmet. Hand it to me. I'll come to get it at second base if you want me to, but don't throw it at my feet. I didn't make the out. Show respect for me." Stuff like that.

He taught me that 30 years ago, and it shows respect. Not only to the manager and coaches, but to the game of baseball. And have you ever seen Cal Jr. throw his helmet?

I think it says a lot. Millions of people watch him not throw a helmet, and I think that makes a statement.

I knew one thing. I never had to tell a player in Baltimore to run a ball out. Not once. Because No. 8 ran everything out. And if No. 8 ran everything out, everybody else ran everything out. And that's what you call leadership.

Not cheerleading, but leadership. Going to the post every single day. Making the game-saving play over and over again. You can count on it. That's a leader. There's a lot of guys who can stand in the dugout and cheer when you're winning, but then when you start losing, you can't find them. Well, Cal Jr. was out front whether we were winning or losing. And that's the best thing that I could say about him, that I could count on him.

Johnny Oates managed 705 games of The Streak while guiding the Baltimore Orioles from 1991 to '94, and he often discussed with Cal possible reasons why The Streak would eventually come to an end. But Oates says he has no clue as to when or how Cal's string of consecutive games played will stop.

"I wouldn't even want to project it," says Oates, the Texas Rangers' skipper since Oct. 19, 1994. "I don't know how it will end. It's a tough call. If Junior thought he was hurting the club, he'd say, 'Don't play me.' But that's the manager's decision — 'Is he hurting the club today?' — which is a tough position to put the manager in.

"Maybe someday Junior will say he's had enough of this and walk in and say, 'I want the day off.' Maybe he won't, I don't know."

Oates shared American League Manager of the Year honors with New York's Joe Torre in 1996 when he guided the Rangers to their first division title in franchise history. He has more than 30 years of experience in professional baseball, including nearly 10 full seasons as a major league catcher with the Orioles, Braves, Phillies, Dodgers and Yankees.

Ken Daley is the national baseball reporter for The Dallas Morning News.

I was only with Cal one year, 1993, and I learned more from him about the game — how to play the game, how to dedicate yourself to the game, how to win the game — than my previous 10 years combined. I wish I had five years with Cal, because he makes everyone around him a better player, a far better player.

The first thing I should try to give folks a feel for is how truly, totally competitive Cal Ripken is. Maybe the best way is to describe how badly he wants to win everything he plays. Never mind baseball, he's that way in whiffle ball.

During rain delays we'd set up a whiffle ball game in the clubhouse, and to determine what was a strike, we'd set up a chair behind the plate. If a guy didn't swing and the pitch hit the chair, then it was a strike. Most guys would be content to hit the back of the chair or the seat. Not Cal. He'd go for a leg, way down. You couldn't hit that pitch ever, but it was a strike. It was how much Cal wanted to beat you.

Remember that Cal is totally dedicated to winning. We'll be talking about that a little later.

When I came to Baltimore, it was like I was walking into a Ripken fire, so to speak. Cal's dad had just been fired as a coach for the Orioles, and his brother Billy had just been released as a player. It was a difficult situation, but one I could identify with to a large degree. I had two older brothers who played, Don with San Diego and Larry with St. Louis. I never got to play with them, but what Cal was going through made me aware of the pain of not getting to play alongside them.

Cal was hurting. But he put it aside like the professional he is, and if anything, he played the game even harder.

I never played with a player who was more demanding, who expected more, of himself and of those around him. As far as understanding the game, he's head and shoulders over anyone else I ever played with. Maybe it was having his father and brother around all that time (that) they drove each other to know more. Whatever it was made Cal the most complete player I've ever seen.

Take a simple pop-up play with runners on. If the ball went to Cal's side of the field, he'd be running out, screaming, "Get behind me!" If the ball was to my side, Cal would start yelling, "Get out there! It's your play!" You have to remember I

Thanks, in part, to countless sessions with his father, Cal set the major league record for highest fielding percentage by a shortstop with a .996 mark in 1990.

Before moving to third in 1997, Cal had hit 345 home runs as a shortstop, the most in major league history and well ahead of second-place Ernie Banks (277). Cal's 855 extra-base hits also topped all short-stops in history.

had just spent three years in Seattle with Junior (Griffey). We'd just stand around and watch him go for everything.

Cal called every hit-and-run defense. I had always called it in Seattle, with the open mouth/closed mouth sign behind your glove, and like everyone else, I tried to be right every time but sometimes I wasn't. Cal was right every time that year. He never screwed up. It got so funny, I'd bet with him he'd be wrong. But he never was.

What he has goes beyond instinct or feel for the game. It's like he's part of the game, totally immersed. It's uncanny.

That year, Ben McDonald, a good righthanded pitcher, had 17 wins. We were partially through the season, when one day, Cal got tired of hearing Ben being given general instructions during conferences on the mound. The orders were always, "Use all your pitches," or "Mix it up."

Cal listened one day, started back to his position, then turned and called (catcher) Chris Hoiles back out and said strongly insisted, "I'll call the pitches." It's a true story. For the rest of the year, from the seventh inning on when Ben pitched, Cal called the pitches from shortstop, hand to hat for a fastball, for instance, to his belt for a breaking ball, his leg for a change. Hoiles just looked to Cal. I can't recall him ever shaking him off.

The next year I was with the Angels and McDonald struck me out to end an inning, and as I walked back to the field, Cal went by me and said, "Who do you think called that pitch?" He was laughing. The next time came I up, I tried to peek out at shortstop without letting anyone see. There was Cal waving at me, laughing again. "I see you trying to peek," he called.

I first met Cal and got to know him a bit at the 1987 All-Star Game. He was wonderful to me, showing me around and all. I had heard so much about his work ethic and all for years. It wasn't until 1993, when I went to spring camp with the Orioles, that I found out it was all true. We had four

Since Cal is practiced at the art of deception, opposing players never can be sure if he's resting, clowning around or actually calling a hit-and-run defensive play.

diamonds at the complex, and Cal ran every morning from diamond to diamond. You hear so much about leading by example. Well, Cal is it.

That spring we had new management, and we were putting in new cutoff and relay plays, and Cal didn't like them since they relied on hearing instructions yelled from behind you on where to line up. Cal insisted we go back to the old way where you had a better view. His rationale was that in spring you could hear easily, but in-season, with 30,000 people yelling during a game, you had to see what was going on. The next day we changed the format using Cal's advice.

He's the real deal, as solid a guy off the field and around the team and community as you've always heard. Often, he'd buy everyone food for team flights: crab cakes if we were leaving Baltimore, salmon if we were in Seattle, something special to each area. It all came out of his pocket. He'd sit and joke and talk baseball, always just one of the guys, everything done with the team in mind.

I remember one night we got killed in Kansas City. Cal knew we had to loosen up some. Next thing, we were back on the field, playing whiffle ball at home plate, only with the game played toward the stands. Guys were out there with Cokes or beer having a great time. We played until 4 a.m., and it worked just like Cal thought it would. We loosened up and everyone played better.

We never talked much about The Streak. It was simple. You just knew from Cal's love of baseball and his desire that if he was coming to the park, he wanted to play, so he played. Almost every day at home, he gets up early, takes his kids to school, goes home and naps a bit and goes to the

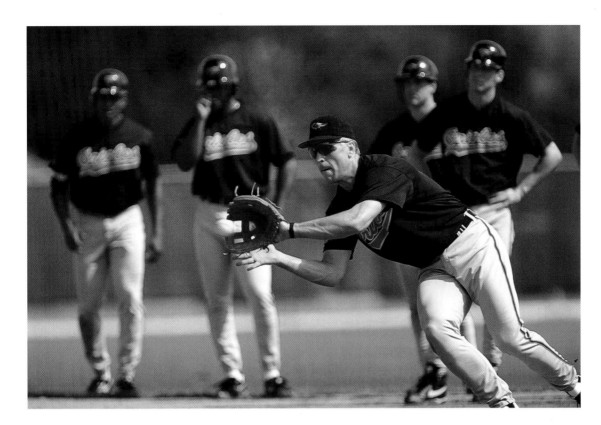

Acutely aware all eyes are on him in games as well as practices, Cal always wears his game face.

park. He just keeps it simple and keeps it going.

I remember when his streak almost ended after the brawl we had with Seattle after Mike Mussina hit Bill Haselman. Cal wound up in the middle of it, of course, and hurt his knee. He told me later it was killing him and he didn't know if he could play.

That night his wife said to him, "Can't you play just one inning, then come out?" Cal said to her, "Not you, too."

The next day he went into the trainer's room and got loose and played. He doesn't buy that DH thing to keep it going, either. He's an infielder, and that's where he plays. In fact, his reluctance to move from short to third was not arrogance or ego. He really felt he did more for the team at short. But now that he's gone to third, he's mastered that position already. He's a great player, one of the greatest

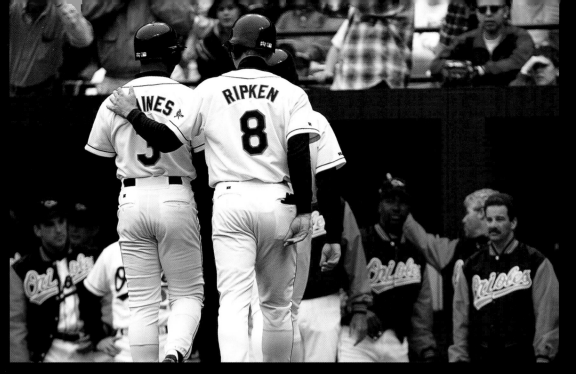

ever. But as I've tried to show, his greatness goes beyond his playing. His dedication and love of baseball are what take him above everyone else.

Harold Reynolds played 10 seasons as a second baseman with the Seattle Mariners before teaming up with Cal Ripken in the Baltimore Orioles' double-play combination for the 1993 season. Reynolds was a two-time American League All-Star (1987 and 1988) and a three-time Gold Glove winner and is still among the Mariners' all-time leaders in games played, runs, hits, doubles, triples, total bases, steals and walks.

He knows what it means for Ripken to play day-in, day-out. In his final five seasons with Seattle, Harold missed just 11 games. From 1987 through 1992, his 932 games played were exceeded in the AL by only Ruben Sierra with 947 games and, by Cal, with 970.

Harold was one of the most popular players of his time, spending more time and money than most players on community and children's charities in Seattle. He became an immediate fan favorite in Baltimore, hosting a Super Bowl Party for 1,000 city teenagers before he even played for the club and sponsoring concerts and other events to raise money for charity.

In 1991 he won the Roberto Clemente Award, presented annually to the player who best exemplifies the game of baseball on and off the field. In 1990 President George Bush presented him with the 195th Daily Point of Light Award, the first athlete to be so honored. He now works as an analyst on ESPN's *Baseball Tonight* program and features reporter on baseball for that network.

Bob Finnigan covers MLB for The Seattle Times.

For one season, 1993, Harold Reynolds contributed to Cal's all-time record of 1,565 double plays turned by a shortstop.

Knowing what Cal has accomplished in baseball isn't lost on me, but for the most part, I only think of him as my son. The one instance where I might have thought of him in another way besides as my son was the night of 2,131.

I might have been removed from the stance of being a mother just a bit because the grandeur of it all was a little much.

That night was like watching something that was unreal. It was fantastic, and probably then I might have inched a little bit away from being a mom.

I'll never forget that night. It was like it wasn't real. All of the commotion . . . the way the crowd reacted. It was like out of a storybook. I don't think anyone could write a script as moving as that one.

Cal and I had conversations beforehand, but I don't think we ever talked about what that day would be like. Cal didn't mention to me what he would say, but I had kind of a warning beforehand.

Ron Shapiro (Ripken's agent) had come up to me and said they were working on this speech. So, I think I was prepared for it, but I didn't know what he would say. It's very rewarding having your son say in a public arena how much he appreciates

"Dad and Mom laid the foundation for my baseball career and my life," Ripken Jr. said during his speech that magical night in Baltimore. Indeed, the Ripkens (from left to right, Cal Jr., wife Kelly, mother Violet and father Cal Sr.) are the most famous family in Maryland.

Violet was always near her son on the night he broke Lou Gehrig's record. Others who honored Cal included former Orioles manager Frank Robinson and the owner of a different kind of impressive streak (the 56-game hitting kind), Joe DiMaggio.

what his parents did for him. I know he's not the only son or daughter who feels that way about his parents . . . they just don't have the opportunity to do it in a public arena.

But, as fantastic as that night was, there have been times when I have wondered what all the fuss is about. I guess that's because of my long association with the game through my husband. I've always thought Cal was doing what he loves to do, and doing what he's paid to do.

Because of that, yes, I wonder what all the fuss is about.

People are always wondering what The Streak

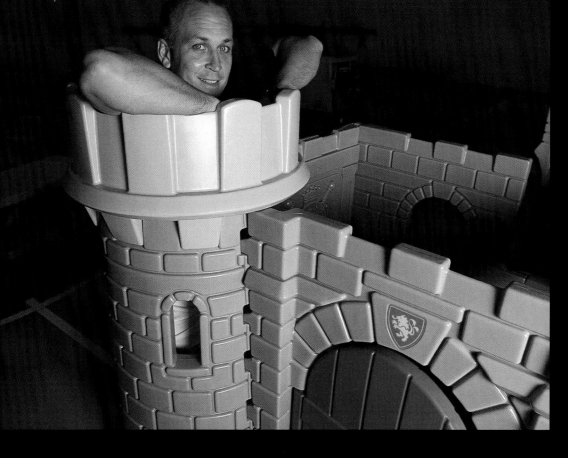

time from workouts to speak with daughter Rachel. Son Ryan was considerate enough to be born on an Orioles' off day during the 1993 season. As a senior in high school, Ripken and his buddies (that's Cal on the right of the photo below) made their marks on the Aberdeen team.

Larger-than-life Cal must seem heaven-sent to Baltimore fans, but fortune hasn't always been on his side during The Streak. There was the time at the 1996 All-Star Game team photo session when Roberto Hernandez slipped and accidentally broke Cal's nose with a backhand. Ripken never missed a beat.

is all about. I think it's about what Cal says it's about. It just means that he's been fortunate enough to stay well, not get hurt, and he has this tremendous desire to be on the field.

Being a baseball player is all I can remember Cal wanting to do. This is what he has always loved.

He always played baseball, but there was no

way you could fathom that it would be like this, even after he got to the big leagues. The big leagues was always his goal, and he made it, but there's no way you could imagine what came afterwards.

I think he was a normal teenage boy growing up. He liked girls, he liked cars and he loved baseball. That makes him a normal teenage boy. I can't say we ever had a lot of trouble with him, other than missing a curfew here and there. I certainly

ON THE 8TH DAY GOD CREATED CAL AND HE HASN'T MISSED A GAME SINCE

Ripken's daughter, Rachel, was born shortly after the 1989 season, just in time to see her father commit just three errors in 161 games the next year. He played 95 straight errorless games that season, one of the many feats that make Cal an excellent endorser for products such as milk.

wouldn't call him rambunctious.

You could never anticipate all this happening. Looking back on him growing up, I saw that he was more focused than some of the other kids, and you can see that trait more as he's gotten older. I've always been asked how he did in school, and there were quite a few years in there when he had perfect attendance.

As a child, he was very meticulous in his thoughts and what he was doing. He had high levels of concentration, and, of course, as an adult that's all been magnified. He certainly hasn't lost any of that as he's gotten older.

I think he got that from his father . . . he did not get that from me.

When Cal was having success, people would say, "It's the father, it's in the genes." I used to say,

Violet taught Cal to eat properly, no doubt contributing to his excellent health since the start of The Streak. Ripken likes to eat at least two meals before even arriving at the ballpark each and every day.

"Wait a minute now, half those genes are mine."

If (Cal Sr.) had met somebody else, there might have been the name, Cal Ripken Jr., but (Cal Jr.) wouldn't have been the same person. I never thought what he specifically got from me and what he got from his father. I just think it's a good combination.

I know how hard Cal has worked to reach this level. I truthfully marvel at the way he handles all of this.

We have had a certain amount of notoriety and being in the public eye, but his is many, many times over what we have had to experience. I marvel at the way he does handle it.

I have no idea what he'll do when he's done playing baseball, but he won't sit back in the rocking chair. I've always said there is life after baseball. I'm sure, knowing him, that he's going through a few things in his mind.

When Cal Ripken Jr. was preparing to leave his home in Aberdeen, Md., to become a professional baseball player, his mother had one piece of advice for him: Learn how to cook.

Since then, Cal has been careful to watch what he eats. The meals of the Iron Man include all the basic food groups, with an emphasis on vegetables. But the influence of Mom goes way beyond Cal's diet. Vi was the guiding force behind the Ripken family, the one who kept the group together despite the road trips and other rigors of professional baseball.

In 1988, The Tops in Sports organization named Violet Ripken "Maryland's First Woman of Baseball," for, in part, having raised sons Cal and Billy to major league teammates with the Baltimore Orioles and being married to Cal Ripken Sr., who spent more than 30 years in the organization.

"I do like the sport," Vi says. "I think if I didn't like the sport, I probably wouldn't have remained married for as long as we have been.

"But after all these years, I don't get caught up in the game as much as I used to."

However, she got caught up in it — as did most of America — on Sept. 6, 1995, when her son broke Lou Gehrig's consecutive games record. That night, Ripken thanked four people for their guidance and support. His mother was one of them.

"What can I say about my mom?" Ripken said. "She is an unbelievable person. She let my dad lead the way on the field, but she was there in every other way — leading and shaping the lives of our family off the field. She's the glue who held our lives together while we grew, and she's always been my inspiration."

John Delcos covers the Orioles for The York (Penn.) Daily Record.

BY THEO CHEN

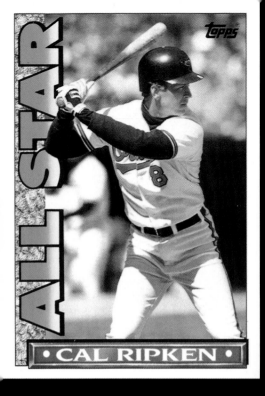

ALL STAR

• CAL RIPKEN •

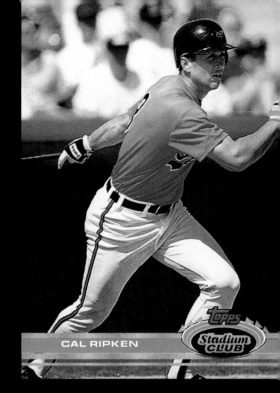

CAL RIPKEN

Topps Stadium CLUB

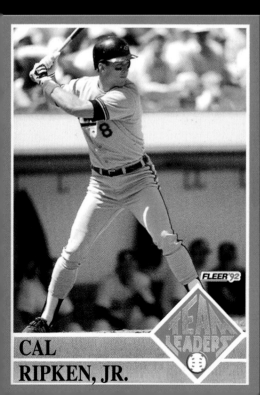

FLEER '92

TEAM LEADERS

CAL RIPKEN, JR.

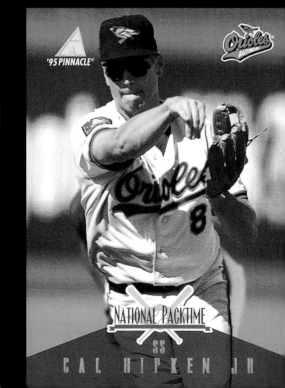

'95 PINNACLE

Orioles Baltimore

National Packtime

SS

CAL RIPKEN JR

I like to think that I'm Cal Ripken Jr.'s biggest fan in the state of Texas. Since I was raised in Maryland, it was only natural that I grew up a fan of the Orioles and Ripken. In 1985, I returned to the hobby after abandoning it as a kid, and wondered why I ever left.

I tried to make up for lost time by building a nice collection of Cal's cards in a three-ring binder. Back then I wanted one of each of his cards, and for his better cards, I wanted more. So I accumulated maybe a dozen Rookie Cards, a few 1982 Topps Tradeds, and five or six of his 1983 Topps second-years and the tougher O-Pee-Chee variety.

In 1989, I moved to Dallas to start working for Beckett, and my collecting habits slowly began shifting from cards to autographs. I still kept up my Cal card collection for several more years, but I increasingly spent more time chasing signatures.

Now that I live in Dallas, I have to travel if I want to see Cal play or have a shot at his autograph more than two series each year. So that's what I do. Not counting All-Star games, I've seen him play in eight American League cities.

In recent years Cal has become not only a bona fide living legend by breaking Lou Gehrig's consecutive games mark, but an unparalleled autograph signing machine at the park. In 1997 alone, I

Chen's passion for collecting Ripken memorabilia began with cards like these (clockwise on opposite page): a '90 Topps TV All-Star; a '91 Topps Stadium Club; a '95 Pinnacle National Packtime and a '92 Fleer Team Leaders insert. Cal's 1992 Topps Traded (above) is the most valuable of his early cards.

got Cal's autograph in five different states, which might be some kind of bizarre record. One of those states was Florida.

During my annual weeklong spring training trips to the Sunshine State, I try to catch at least a couple of O's games. One in particular, an afternoon game in late March 1997 at Vero Beach, I'll never forget.

It was a humid 90 degrees. The Orioles wore those heat-absorbing, sweat-inducing black spring training road uniforms. After being lifted in the seventh inning, Cal ran countless laps along the warning track. The game ended. Time for him to leave? Not quite.

The hype from his historic 2,131 season of 1995 had long since passed. The ill will caused by the 1994 work stoppage had all but dissipated. I saw the other players blow off fans like they weren't even there. Cal could get away with devoting less time to signing, and no one would say a bad word about him.

Besides, before the game he signed for a good 20 minutes along the Dodgers' side of the field. But there were fans piled five-deep on the visitors' side. Sure enough, Cal headed behind the aluminum benches that serve as the dugouts in Dodgertown and started to sign. And sign. And sign some more.

He signed baseball cards. Black bats. White bats. Eight-by-10 photos. Magazines. Programs. Jerseys. T-shirts. Wheaties boxes. Baseballs of every color and style. Ceramic plates. Posters. Gloves. Homemade signs. Artwork ranging from a

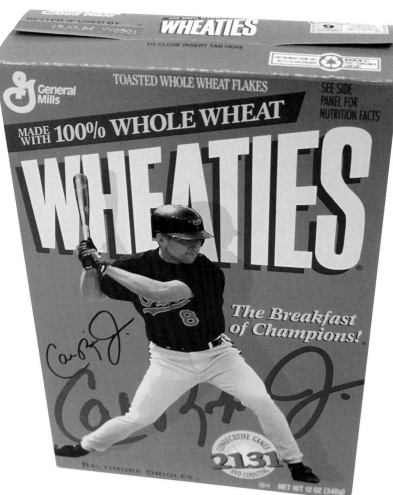

professional lithograph to a child's pencil scrawling. Batting helmets. Caps. Kenner Starting Lineups. The fans came at him in endless waves, a sea of outstretched arms thrusting items toward him while a cacophony of voices chanted his name.

Cal carefully took each item and studied it for a second. He looked for the best place to sign, tested the pen if necessary, and inscribed his perfect signature. Every now and again he exchanged a greeting, a thank-you-you're-welcome.

I'm sure he knew a significant percentage of these items would be offered for sale almost before the ink dried. I guess being the class act that he is, he doesn't concern himself with that.

The thought crossed my mind that in his one postgame autograph session, he'd already spent more time obliging fans than some major league teams do in a full day of spring training, or more than many individual players do during the entire month of March.

Advice to autograph seekers: Cal will notice, and be more likely to sign, an unusual item like this Wheaties box during a crowded signing session.

About 90 minutes after the game ended, Cal had finally signed his way down to the end of the first base line, but the masses were still there, screaming his name.

I somehow fought my way in, and stretched my arm out as far as it would go. In my hand I had an orange-and-black Spinneybeck baseball and a

silver paint pen. I could see Cal was soaked in sweat, and his left hand was dotted with ink marks of every color from testing pens. In his right hand he held a blue ball point pen.

Cal took my baseball and paint pen, looked at me and asked, "Blue on the orange, silver on the orange, or silver on the black?" I replied, "Silver on the orange, please." Cal slowly signed it and handed it back to me, obviously taking care not to smear the fresh signature.

By now Cal was just yards away from his sport utility vehicle, which he drove up from Fort Lauderdale knowing the team bus would be long gone by the time he left the park. Still, he continued to oblige his fans.

Finally, after signing literally hundreds of perfect autographs, it was time to go. He tried and tried, but he couldn't get to everyone. It seems that

As Cal's physical appearance has changed through the years, so has his autograph. Notice the difference in the "J" from his early jersey and cap to the Spinneybeck baseball Chen had signed in March '97.

the more he signs, the more people show up wanting his signature. That's the way it goes.

I was so elated by my special moment with Cal that only a few minutes later did I realize just how surreal the whole exchange was. After signing for 90 minutes, Cal still took the time to give me three options on how I wanted my baseball signed. Sometimes you don't get that kind of service when you're paying for an autograph at a card show!

It's a good thing I was there in Vero Beach that day, because if I had heard about it second-hand, I might not have believed it. Each time I see Cal, I become a bigger fan of his, but this particular scene just blew me away.

The devoted signature collector that I am, I've become a bit cynical when it comes to celebrity autograph attitudes. Believe me, I've heard every excuse imaginable. When Bobby Bonilla was with Baltimore, he'd often decline requests by pointing in Cal's direction and sarcastically uttering, "Iron Man's over there."

When I think of Cal, I think, "no excuses." That's the way he approaches the game, and that's the way he treats fans. I don't know where he gets the patience and stamina. I can't speak for the

thousands of Cal collectors out there, but in a nutshell, that's why I collect his memorabilia with such a passion.

By the time Cal was in striking distance of Gehrig's 2,130 consecutive games mark, I knew I had to be there in person when he broke it, or I'd never forgive myself.

You may recall that the start of the 1995 season was postponed by labor strife. That put Cal's big night on hold indefinitely. The day after the settlement, when the new schedule was announced, I got out my calendar and counted the days until projected games 2,130 (Sept. 5) and 2,131 (Sept. 6), home games against the Angels. I called and ordered tickets. For 2,130 I got front row in the right field corner, but 2,131 was sold out already.

In case of rainouts, I ordered tickets to the next series at Cleveland. Then I bought plane tickets to Baltimore and Cleveland. I decided to hold off on the Sept. 6 ticket chase until I was pretty sure it would happen.

When September finally came, I called ticket brokers until I found the lowest price, which was $175, and hesitated only briefly before pulling the trigger. On one hand, $175 seemed an absurd markup on a $14 face value ticket; on the other hand, $175 seemed a potential bargain for the experience of a lifetime.

In retrospect, I would gladly have paid double that price had I known just how memorable it would be. Games 2,130 and 2,131 easily surpassed all previous baseball events I've experienced before or since, including six All-Star games, six World Series games and Nolan Ryan's 5,000th strikeout and seventh no-hitter.

Cal always takes the time to pick the most attractive spot for his signature, no matter how frenzied the situation.

This commemorative plate captures the spirit of Sept. 6, 1995, when Cal broke the supposedly unbreakable record.

Despite the incredible hoopla and attention, Ripken attempted to maintain his normal pregame schedule on both games — which included signing for fans along the home dugout side. In fact, I was lucky enough to get his autograph on Sept. 5.

The jubilation and outpouring of emotion in Camden Yards those two nights are permanently etched in my memory. And like just about everyone else who was there, I was caught up in the frenzy for memorabilia and souvenirs.

Years later, it's still impossible to list all the 2,131-related collectibles produced, but here are some of the most interesting and coveted.

• Game tickets for both Sept. 5 and 6 were not torn at the gates but embossed with a special Ripken 2,130/2,131 logo designed by the Orioles for the event. The embossing is difficult to see on light-colored tickets.

Mint (but embossed) 2,131 tickets now sell in the $150-$250 range, with 2,130 tickets bringing

Sept. 6. A paper insert describes the "Streak Week" activities. They sold out at $3 nonetheless and now are valued at $20 to $30.

• On Sept. 5, the Orioles released the Cal Ripken Official Commemorative Book, which many people confused as a program. The softcover book is filled with beautiful color photos. Despite a limit of five per person, the books sold out at $10 inside the stadium on both days, although they were available for the rest of the season in Camden Yards and through mail order. They now sell for $12 to $20.

• Fans attending the Sept. 6 game received a foldout poster as they walked in. The front features the Ripken 2,130/2,131 logo, the back details in tiny type the date, opponent and score of all 2,130 games. Inside are two color photos: one from Game 1 (May 30, 1982), one from game 2,130. The poster is now valued at $25 to $40.

• The American League authorized Rawlings

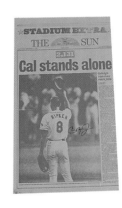

The Sept. 7 edition of the *Baltimore Sun* is valued at $10 to $20, but the aluminum printers plates are more valuable and durable, which makes them better for autographs.

about half that. What a deal — my $175 ticket to 2,131 is worth more than that now, and I got to experience the event!

When the gates opened on Sept. 5, some of the ticket-takers were obliging requests to emboss items other than tickets. When the lines to get in got too long, this was discontinued.

• The Orioles did not produce a special program for the games, but the program available was for the entire nine-game homestand that ended on

to produce special commemorative baseballs to be used during those two games only. This was the first time in history that commemorative balls were used in regular season games. They feature orange laces and the 2,130/2,131 logo.

A limited number of the special baseballs sold out at $20 almost immediately both days. Rawlings announced that the original supply was limited by a shortage of orange lace, and the company assured fans more baseballs were on the way.

Today, the orange baseballs are fairly plentiful and sell for about $15. Should you be so lucky as to get a 2,130/2,131 ball signed by Ripken, you have a $90-$120 item.

• The main Baltimore post office offered a special commemorative postmark on Sept. 6 only. Fans could get anything they wanted postmarked, which explains why they began lining up early in

This commemorative book was a hot seller in Camden Yards during "Streak Week" as collectors scrambled for 2,131 memorabilia.

the morning. Both Gateway and Historic Limited Edition, the leading sports commemorative cachet producers, issued envelopes for 2,131.

• The *Baltimore Sun* produced a special stadium edition that quickly sold out outside Camden Yards after the Sept. 6 game. Many fans were seen carrying away stacks of 20 or more papers. The regular morning editions of the Sept. 6 *Sun* and *Washington Post* contained special Ripken sections. While all area papers obviously had extensive coverage on Sept. 7, the *Washington Times* also included a Ripken color poster.

The Sept. 7 morning *Baltimore Sun*, with both front page and sports page dominated by Ripken's feat, now is valued at $10 to $20.

I have most of the aforementioned items, and my 2,131 collection still takes up a lot of space. But it's worth it. It carries so much meaning for me.

I still have my Cal card binder stuffed full, even though I've rarely added to it since 1995. Most of the cards Cal has signed for me over the years are in my safety deposit box; the bigger stuff is either on display or waiting to be framed.

Fellow hobbyists often ask me, "Haven't you gotten enough Cal stuff already?" My answer, of course, is no. Someday I'd like to get a signed game-used bat or jersey — the closest thing I have now is a signed unused bat issued to Ripken around 1991. I'd also like to be in attendance for his final game, and I'd like to be in Cooperstown to hear his Hall of Fame induction speech.

I think that day, hopefully many years in the future, will close the book on my Cal collection. But my collection will forever give me pleasant memories of Sept. 6, 1995, and countless other ordinary games when I watched Cal display his usual class, determination and excellence.

Theo Chen is the Price Guide editor of *Future Stars/Beckett Sports Collectibles* and also writes an "In Person" autograph column for the monthly magazine, one of seven sports card and memorabilia hobby guides produced by Beckett Publications.

While he considers himself the biggest Cal fan and collector in the Lone Star State, he defers to people such as Bill Haelig, Don Harrison and Dave "Ironfan" Peterson for national honors. Of his 30 or so Ripken autographs, Chen's favorite is the game-model bat he bought at a Brian McRae charity auction in Kansas City that he finally got autographed in April 1997, more than five years after he acquired it.

THE ROOKIE

BY EARL WEAVER AS TOLD TO JOE STRAUSS

There was no question that Cal was going to be part of our team in '82. The only issue was whether he would begin the season at third base or at shortstop. The organization was afraid of Doug DeCinces' back. There was some doubt about whether he could hold up for an entire season because he had missed 20 or 30 games the year before. Rip was coming out of the minor leagues as a third baseman, and the club thought Doug might be dispensable.

There was a lot of talk about dealing DeCinces. Really and truthfully, I was against a trade. I wanted to play Rip at shortstop and DeCinces at third. I believed DeCinces could give us 25 to 30 home runs and felt Ripken probably would hit 20 homers, which would give me 45 home runs or so from the left side of the infield. Not many clubs could say that.

But the organization was hesitant about committing to that. Eventually, DeCinces was traded to the California Angels for Don Aase, a solid reliever who ended up helping the club for a couple years.

The trade itself was a good one because we had found a solid closer. But Doug came out and hit around 30 home runs for the Angels and Rip wound up at shortstop anyway.

There was never a question Cal would be an outstanding player. But like all rookies, he got off to a slow start. What he needed most was time. Unfortunately, he got off to his slow start at third base, which is an offensive position. We were struggling for runs at the time and a decision was made to move him to shortstop, which would take some pressure off him to produce.

Cal had played shortstop in high school. His dad had been a coach for me and sometimes brought Cal to the ballpark to take ground balls. He had a great arm and pitched a couple no-hitters in high school. He had all the ability to play short.

Our regular shortstop, Bobby Bonner, wasn't hitting, either, and wasn't playing good defensive

Cal Ripken Jr.'s 23 homers in his only season with the Triple-A Rochester Red Wings earned him an August 1981 call-up to Baltimore, where he joined Earl Weaver and the big-league Orioles.

After homering a combined eight times in his first two seasons in the minors, Ripken went deep 25 times for Charlotte in 1980, earning him attention from the media along with a spot on the Southern League All-Star team.

ball. In order to get offense in the lineup, I moved Cal over and put Floyd Rayford at third base.

I knew it was just a matter of time until Cal began to hit. He was young and needed to get through the league the first time to become comfortable. For whatever reason, things seemed to work against Cal playing shortstop.

When he went to the minor leagues he was a 17-year-old kid and, naturally, made a lot of throwing errors at Bluefield (the Orioles' Rookie Advanced team). Then the organization signed a 21-year-old kid out of Texas. Simply because of the age difference, he was head and shoulders above Cal at that time, so they put Cal at third and this

kid at shortstop.

The kid never advanced beyond what he had been in college.

I knew Cal wasn't going to be a 50 home run guy. But I had the advantage of watching his father bring him out early some days for infield and batting practice. He was hitting balls out of Memorial Stadium when he was 15 and 16 years old. The potential was always there. It was simply a matter of adjusting.

When Cal went to shortstop, he had absolutely no trouble. Offensively, he had to get around the league. It was my job to judge talent, and in my opinion, he had tremendous talent.

He did everything everybody expected him to do. He hit 28 home runs, hit around .264 and did a fantastic job at shortstop. He's always had sure hands. What people didn't fully appreciate was how much range Cal had for his size. He covered a tremendous amount of ground. I watched (former St. Louis shortstop) Marty Marion and his reach was tremendous. Cal was like that. Where a little shortstop took five steps, Cal got there in two.

For Cal, there was very little adjustment to a major league clubhouse. He'd grown up there. Guys expect you to come in and do your job. Once you do your job, there's no adjusting. You play nine innings, you go home. The team knew he was a good player. Everyone knew he had tremendous talent.

When you're a rookie, you either prove yourself or you go back to Triple-A. A lot of guys get sent back to the minors. Mickey Mantle went back. Ted Williams went back. The adjustment to the pitching is tremendous, and Cal had some problems. But with his background, his ability and his intensity, you knew he was going to be all right once he got through the league once.

In my mind, you stay with a guy until he at least goes through the league once, even if he's hitting .180. Cal didn't surprise me. Managing is baseball judgment — who can do what and when.

"Even (in the minors), he seemed to know what was going to happen in the games," says Jimmy Williams, who coached Cal for four minor league seasons. "We'd go into a room, and he'd be talking with coaches who'd been in the game more than 30 years like he was one of them."

Cal made his major league debut the first game after the players strike was settled in 1981. Ripken saw his first action as a pinch runner after Ken Singleton led off the 12th inning of a game against Kansas City with a double. Cal came around to score the winning run on John Lowenstein's single.

As the AL Rookie of the Year in 1982, Cal led all major league rookies in doubles, homers, RBI, total bases, at-bats and runs. He sat out of just three games that year before May 30, when he started The Streak that would continue to 2,131 consecutive games 13 years later.

If your judgment is good and you pick the right 25 guys for your roster, then you're going to win. If you pick the wrong 25 guys, you're going to lose.

You have organizational meetings to go over what you're going to need. You grade all the players around the league and determine what you have and what's available. At some point, you tell the general manager, "This guy is going to make it. I want him on the team." There was never any doubt in my mind that Cal was going to make it.

What he's accomplished is unbelievable. Certainly, no one could have anticipated The Streak. That's a once-in-a-lifetime thing. But what he's done on the field . . . I would have been shocked if he hadn't become an outstanding, All-Star-caliber player.

Of course, he's been that, and more.

Earl Weaver managed the Orioles from 1968 through 1982, and again from 1985 to '86. Inducted into the Baseball Hall of Fame in 1996, Weaver ranks 17th in victories among managers this century. His winning percentage of .583 ranks fifth among managers with 10 or more seasons in the 20th century.

Through 17 seasons, all with Baltimore, Earl won

1,480 games. His teams won six AL East titles, including three straight from 1969 to 1971, and four American League pennants. His 1970 team won the World Series in five games over Cincinnati.

After retiring following the 1982 season, during which his team finished one game behind the Milwaukee Brewers in the division race, Weaver returned in the middle of the 1985 season for a year and-a-half before retiring for good. That last season of 1986 was the only time his team posted a losing record.

Weaver spent most of his 13-year minor league playing career at second base in the St. Louis Cardinals organization. He began his managing career in the minors in 1956, joined the Orioles organization a year later and finally broke into the big leagues as a first base coach in 1968.

Joe Strauss covers the Orioles for The Baltimore Sun.

By now, I guess everyone has heard that my admiration for Cal Ripken started when I was a kid and that I had a poster of him hanging over my bed. It's true. Somehow it came out it was a life-size poster. It's big, but not that big. He was my favorite player. And although I have deep respect for a number of players on our Mariners team — Junior (Griffey), Jay (Buhner), Edgar (Martinez) — I think they'll understand when I say Cal is still my favorite.

I can't remember exactly when it started, but I do know why. Actually, I had three players I liked when I was real little: Cal, of course, and Dale Murphy and Keith Hernandez. I guess I liked them because they worked hard. Not only were they everyday players, and star players, but they worked to keep their status.

As I played more shortstop, Cal became my favorite because he was also a shortstop. He did exactly what I wanted to do by establishing himself early. He won the Rookie of the Year (1982) and Most Valuable Player his second year (1983) to help his Baltimore team go to the World Series and win the championship.

He was the only shortstop I knew of that hit third in the lineup. That was almost fake, like he was too good to be true. Shortstops are defensive guys, little hitters. They sometimes hit near the top of the order if they're good hitters but don't have power. They're usually near the bottom, because their defense is better than any part of their offense.

I had power. I hit third. I was growing up to be bigger than most kids who play shortstop. It seemed I was going to get as big as Cal — he's 6-4

and I'm 6-3 now — and that was a link between us in my mind. On top of all that, Cal never showboated. He just played hard all the time, and from everything I heard, was good people off the field and did a lot of good works in the community. Also there was that thing about playing every day, and to me, that is the epitome of professionalism, to go to war every day in, day out.

To this day, I get embarrassed thinking about the first time I got an opportunity to meet Mr. Ripken at an Orioles' spring training game. There was this man named Mario, who was a huge fan of Westminster, my high school in Miami. I remember

As a high school phenom in Miami, Rodriguez dreamed of being like Cal. In '97, the 21-year-old made history by being the first AL All-Star not named Ripken Jr. to start at short in 14 years.

he called me one morning when I was a sophomore. It had to be a Saturday or spring break, because I was still asleep at 9 o'clock. He asked me if I wanted to go to a game in Ft. Lauderdale. This was after the Orioles left Miami, and I never got to go to a game there because my mom wouldn't let me go. I was a kid, and the Miami park was in kind of a rough area of town.

Anyway, Mario picked me up, and we drove up to Ft. Lauderdale. It was a Baltimore-St. Louis

game. Our seats were in the stands in back of the plate, and I sat there while Mario went down near the field to see Johnny Oates, who was a friend of his and the Orioles' manager. I remember sitting up there dying and hoping I could meet Cal, but worrying that Mario would say something that would embarrass me.

Next thing, Mario was calling me down to meet Johnny. When I got to them, Mario introduced me and said, "This is the kid who would like to meet Cal." Johnny said he had heard good things about me. He was so nice to me, and it's one reason I really like John. But I was so shy, I never even made eye contact with him.

Then Cal came into the dugout to go out and take infield for the game. Johnny called him over. I was dying, yet I was in heaven already. I remember really having goose bumps, real goose bumps. He stuck his hand out to shake mine and said, "I've heard good things about you." I didn't realize, but he had read an SI (Sports Illustrated) story that predicted I was a future No. 1 pick in the draft. It was only a 30-second meeting, but I remember every second of it. To be honest, one reason I remember it is Cal never lets me forget it. He makes fun of the way I was — real "Duh" — that day.

When I first came to the majors in 1994, I remember wishing it had come when the team was in Baltimore so I could meet Cal again. The Mariners made the decision when they were there but left and went to Boston, where I joined them. But I had a couple of chances to talk to him over the next couple of years, and then, at the end of the 1996 season, I was asked to join a major league

Cal's 34 home runs in 1991 stood as the most by a shortstop since 1969 (when Boston's Rico Petrocelli hit 40) until Rodriguez blasted 36 homers in 1996.

tour of Japan. They had asked a National League shortstop to go and Cal was going for the American League. But the NL guy couldn't go and they asked me. I really didn't want to. After the 1996 season I had, I really only wanted to relax. But this would give me a chance to spend time with Cal, and I jumped at that.

Going to Japan and spending time with Cal every day was like a man off the street getting to go to a fantasy camp with Jay or Junior. I was going to platoon with Cal Ripken, my all-time favorite player. I was going to get a chance to pick his brain. Wow. Yet, you know, I was worried about one thing. I had put Rip on a pedestal, and now I was going to find out if he was really that kind of person. I had such big expectations, you know?

For 11 days Cal was everything I had thought he would be, hoped he would be. We spent time together every day, shared so much. I learned so much about professionalism, discipline, timeliness.

If he wants to field like his idol, Alex has a ways to go. In Cal's nearly flawless season of 1990, he set three major league records for shortstops: fielding percentage (.996), consecutive chances without an error (431) and consecutive errorless games (90).

Just watching him carry himself you learn the right way to do things.

The best time was one night coming back from some function that had gone late after a game. We shared a cab at 4 a.m., and later at the hotel, we sat and talked until 5:30. We talked about everything: baseball, life, marriage. How great was it? The only comparison I can think of would be if a music fan got to talk with Elvis like that. He's such a real person, an honorable man and a proud player. He's usually a private person, but he shared a lot with me and helped me a lot in so many ways.

Among the things Cal taught me were a couple of ways he likes to make specific plays. On the play up the middle, for instance, if you take the ball behind you, make the full 360 (degree) turn for momentum to make a throw to first. But if you take the ball in front of you, you can curl inside, twist

Few people realize the dream of rubbing shoulders (and trading elbows) with the people they admire most. Even fewer have the potential to approach the heady heights achieved by their idols.

your body to change momentum and make a throw. The throw won't be as hard, but the time saved from not turning makes up for that.

Then on the chopper over the mound, instead of taking the ball off the left shoulder as usual, he tries to get there quick enough to take the ball off his right shoulder. He brought this up to me after I missed getting a fast player in Japan, a guy named Ichiro who has speed like (Texas Rangers center fielder) Tom Goodwin in our league. I took the ball off my left shoulder and was late. Cal pointed out if I can get the ball off the right shoulder, I'm taking it in throwing position already and don't have to twist and get throwing position. It's lots quicker.

One thing that immediately came from the Japan trip was an invitation for me to come to Cal's house outside Baltimore and work out with him in his weight room and play basketball with

It's probably a sure bet that Seattle's rising star is the only hard-core collector of Ripken memorabilia who has slid under Cal's tag or gone deep into the hole to steal a hit from the Iron Man.

him and his friends on the court he has right in his house. I was honored. Not many get included like this. He's unbelievably good at basketball, too, just a really good athlete. I like to think I'm a good player, but this was good competition. He's sound fundamentally, works hard on defense — of course — and uses his body well. He generally plays bigger than his height.

I've already had a lot of good things come to me in my major league time, but one of the sweetest was getting voted in as American League All-Star shortstop (in 1997) and getting to play next to Cal in the infield. He moved to third and was voted to start there. When the game was starting, I looked over to my right, and there he was. It was unbelievable to me. I thought to myself to try to take a picture in my mind to hold there forever, because you sometimes forget the great moments in your life, and this was definitely one of mine. In fact, though, I don't have any pictures of us side-by-side on the infield in that game, and if anyone has one, I would like a copy if they get in touch with me. I'll never forget the sight and feel of the game, but a real picture would be great.

I have other pictures of Cal and me together, tons of them, all personalized. I have one of his bats, signed. The next thing I'm hoping to get is one of his jerseys. If that sounds like a typical fan, I guess that's because I am a fan of Cal's even though we've become friends, too.

And just like anyone else would, I had to ask him about The Streak. How? Why? He told me he never meant for it to get like this, that he had played three or four straight years and suddenly people started calling it a streak. He has played hurt at times, he has played with injuries, but obviously nothing that bad. But it's not about The Streak. It's simply that he likes to play, and he has an ethic that makes him earn his pay every day, like Junior and Jay here in Seattle. I admire so much about him on the field and off, but his work ethic is the part of him I like best.

I still have that poster of him. Remember how I said I knew it wasn't life-size? It's 20 inches by 16 inches. I know that because I had it framed. It's not over my bed anymore. When we moved my mom into a new house in Miami, we hung that poster in a place of honor in the hallway.

Seattle's Alex Rodriguez became the American League's starting All-Star shortstop in 1997 for two reasons: First, he won the league batting championship with a .358 average while setting a number of all-time

marks for shortstops in his first full season in 1996. Second, Cal Ripken moved to third after being an AL All-Star shortstop for 14 years.

Rodriguez's admiration for Ripken is sincerely reciprocated. Ripken, an intensely private man, is wary about sitting for interviews with the press. When in 1996 a Seattle reporter requested some of his time, through Baltimore PR man John Maroon, Cal turned it down with his usual polite firmness.

When Cal learned the reporter wanted only Ripken's thoughts about Alex Rodriguez, Ripken immediately suggested a time that day. He was fun and insightful, recalling one play in Camden Yards in which Rodriguez made a difficult play, righted himself and threw the ball, "about 1,000 miles an hour," for the out. "I looked down the dugout and my brother Billy was looking back at me," Cal said. "We kind of raised our eyebrows and nodded to each other. We knew. This kid is something special."

Bob Finnigan covers the Mariners for The Seattle Times.

HOMETOWN HERO

BY JON MILLER

Y ou have your choice of memories with Cal Ripken. It's a vast and impressive selection. Pick a year. Pick a month. Pick a game. Pick an instance. But there's one we all share with him readily — that night in Baltimore.

And where else? If he was ever going to do it, if he was ever going to break the record that couldn't be broken, he had to do it at home. It had to be in Baltimore. Another city would have appreciated the accomplishment, of course. As it turned out, all of baseball appreciated what he did as an achievement and as a significant step in healing the game and adding to its lore. But no other city could appreciate Cal Ripken the way Baltimore did. And still does.

In and around Baltimore, a city once dubbed "the biggest small town in America" and grounded on a strong industrial and maritime tradition, citizens can relate with Cal's tremendous work ethic.

Unlike legends such as Joe DiMaggio, who was a hero in the Pacific Coast League before he joined the Yankees, and Michael Jordan, whose exploits in college at North Carolina made him famous, Cal Ripken Jr.'s fame is rooted in Baltimore.

He came from Baltimore, lived in Baltimore and never left. His roots run deeper than Chesapeake Bay. Deny Baltimore its Cal Ripken, and you deny the city its crab cakes. That moment and that man are now part of the city in a way that perhaps exceeds the way Joe DiMaggio is part of New York, the way Joe Montana is part of the Bay Area and the way Michael Jordan is part of Chicago.

The difference is that Cal is Baltimore. Rooted there. Pete Rose was that way in Cincinnati — hometown hero. But Cal is about family in Baltimore baseball. The city knew he was coming. It could watch him grow. There was a Cal Ripken who most folks knew and liked before there was a Cal Ripken Jr. to take the relationship another step, and as it turned out, to another level.

His whole identity is Baltimore. DiMaggio was a star in the Pacific Coast League when that league was like a third major league, before he played an inning in New York. Montana was the quarterback for the most storied collegiate football program in the country (Notre Dame) before he threw a pass for the 49ers. Jordan was an All-American at North Carolina before he ever slam-dunked for the Bulls.

Cal was an Oriole even before he played for them. We saw the seed. We thought he had an idea about what the flower might be. I think we underestimated its beauty and staying power.

Pete had similar status in Cincinnati, and they would end up naming a street after him. But now there are parts of Pete's career that, rightly or wrongly, have stained his reputation. And Pete didn't have the same degree of recognition in Cincinnati that Cal had before he made it to the big leagues. Pete was Pete. Cal was Cal's son, Cal Jr. He was "Cal" primarily. And you used the "Junior" out of respect for his father and as a means to distinguish between the two. So he was Cal Senior's son and Billy's brother and the player chasing Gehrig and the MVP and the guy who played every day. He gave the city so many ways to connect with him.

The influence of the family connection can't be underestimated in Cal becoming the hometown hero. Because it's a small city, Baltimore just feels like family. Most everyone has the same issues to deal with because most everyone is from the same "family." I know when the switch from shortstop to third (in 1996) became a topic, it was the only topic on the radio. And it wasn't just your stereotypical hardcore Orioles fans weighing in. It was women and teenage girls. What was happening to their "brother" Cal.

Remember, Baltimore didn't have a football team for a while. The NBA and the NHL were in

The Kelly and Cal Ripken Jr. Foundation, run by the player and his wife, supports community adult and family literacy and youth recreational programs in the greater Baltimore area. Cal is also involved with such programs as The Baltimore Reads Ripken Learning Center and Reading, Runs and Ripken.

Washington, D.C. The Orioles were the city's team. Cal was the team's focal point. He was everyone's big brother.

Families tend to stay in Baltimore generation after generation. I remember Cal had a relative who played baseball but never made it. He was offered a job, a good job, in a bank. But it would have taken him away from Baltimore. He turned it down. Didn't want to leave.

And there's the baseball family too. Cal's part of it. You go back to Brooks Robinson and Mark Belanger and then Boog Powell and Eddie Murray. Cal was born into that family because of his dad. He was in spring training when he was a kid. He was around the game all his life. He had a lot of brothers. I remember him picking Belanger's mind about

how to position himself, leaning on Mark like he was the big brother. We all watched that develop, the whole city watched it. We saw Cal coming, like a small town watches the senior quarterback's brother grow up and develop.

Cal's part of the fabric now, as readily associated with the city as any person. Who knows? If they created a new city flag for Baltimore with scenes depicting the history of the city, Cal might warrant a place on it.

Cal made his mark on Baltimore turf, playing for a Baltimore team, in a new Baltimore ballpark. And you figure the team and the ballpark are going to stay around for a long time. So will Cal, and not just because of the ballpark and the team. When

through 1997, Cal Sr.
and brother Billy had
combined to hit 390
home runs. The duo
played for Cal Sr.
from 1987-'88. But
in high school, Cal
(front row, third from
left in team photo)
was known more
for his pitching at
Aberdeen (Md.) High.
He was 7-2 with a
0.70 ERA his senior
year of 1978, during
which he struck out
100 batters in just
60 innings.

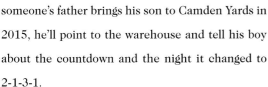

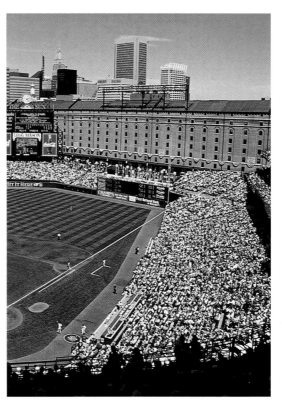

The old Memorial Stadium (left) was certainly a fine place to watch a ball game, but nothing compares to "The House that Cal Built," Oriole Field at Camden Yards (right), where Ripken helped save the game of baseball with his record-breaking 2,131 performance.

someone's father brings his son to Camden Yards in 2015, he'll point to the warehouse and tell his boy about the countdown and the night it changed to 2-1-3-1.

That boy can tell his boy 20 years later . . . if the warehouse is still there. That's how legends become legends. Cal has become one of the few players whose identity adds to the ballpark while the ballpark adds to his identity. It's why people don't want to see old parks torn down.

You can't point anymore to where Aaron's 715th went, or where Mays made the catch against Vic Wertz. Or where Kiner hit his home runs. Or where Mickey's ball hit the façade.

Now Oriole Park has one of those moments. They made it a great place to watch a game. He made it greater. And what he did and how it was saluted that night just enhanced the ballpark. Then

and for the future.

"The House that Cal Built" might be a little too much, a little presumptuous. He might feel awkward about that. Probably would. But you could make a case for it. Ruth helped save the game after the Black Sox (scandal of 1919) by hitting home runs, and he made the Yankees the franchise. Cal helped the game heal after the strike in '94 by playing every day. And what's delicious about all that is that they're both connected to Gehrig. There's a link.

Baseball is all about links. Ruth to Gehrig to DiMaggio to Mantle, Mays to McCovey to Bobby Bonds to Barry Bonds. Brooks to Boog to Eddie Murray to Cal. We get to know more about our baseball heroes because the game is played every day. There's a story in the newspaper every day from the middle of February to the end of October, or at least the end of September. And if you're the

Think Aberdeen, Md., is proud of its native son? The Ripken Museum encourages visitors to learn more about Cal's accomplishments.

man on your team, and if you play your career in that one city, you can't help but become known.

DiMaggio was private. Murray was private. We feel we know them probably better than we feel we know the once-a-week football player. Even the quarterbacks. They're judged once a week, 16 times a year. In baseball, your performance is evaluated every day, 162 times a year.

And in Cal's case, it has been exactly 162 times a year. He has been on the field every inning. There are many fans who never have seen an inning of Orioles baseball without seeing Cal at shortstop or now at third.

Part of his appeal in Baltimore and the respect the city has for him lie within the routine of every day. Baltimore is a working-class town. There's no Park Avenue, Lakeshore Drive. A city of people who work every day. They connect to Cal that way. They go to work every day at 7 or 9 in the morning. He's there every night at 7:35. There's a sense of security in that. Turn on the TV at 8, and within a few minutes you'll catch a glimpse of him. He's there more often now than Cronkite was, and a lot more than Carson was.

You can't overstate the impact. Like the traffic cop or the crossing guard who's there every day, rain or shine, waving to everyone. He's part of the scene. The familiarity is comforting. You think he'll be there forever.

In Cal's case, it almost seems that he has been.

During Jon Miller's broadcasting stint in Baltimore, he — like so many other fans — never saw an Orioles game without Cal Ripken at third or short. That included The Night, when Miller was the master of ceremonies for the postgame celebration.

"Cal broke the record, he broke Lou Gehrig's record, and in the process, he gave so many of us a marker in time," remembered Miller, an Orioles broadcaster from 1983 to 1996. "You know where you were that night. You know where you were when they put 2,131 up on the warehouse, just like you know where you were when you heard when President Kennedy had been killed, or when you heard about Princess Diana. How many times do you experience one of those moments when the memory is so purely positive?"

Miller currently serves as the radio and television voice of the San Francisco Giants, when he's not doing play-by-play for ESPN's *Sunday Night Game of the Week*. He has been nominated for cable ACE awards four times and won an ACE in 1990 for his play-by-play work.

Marty Noble covers professional baseball for New York's Newsday.

For the entire week before, I remember practicing my speech in the outfield during pitching changes. I had it memorized, but I read it anyway. I didn't want to take any chances. I practiced with my mom, but nobody else knew I was doing it. I didn't tell anybody. I didn't want people asking, "Are you nervous?" or stuff like that. I remember thinking about being nervous, and after all the buildup finally saying, "I don't know what you're worried about. You know how to read, so go do it." I wasn't nervous after that.

I remember a lot of things about that night, but some of the things that stand out most are things people couldn't know about. I remember (Shawn) Boskie was pitching and that I wanted to get a hit. I hit two home runs in the game (Cal) tied (Lou Gehrig's record).

I knew the box scores would be showing up everywhere until the end of time, and I wanted a hit next to my name. I lined a single to left and got my obligatory hit.

I remember something somebody had written about Cal . . . about him saying he would go 1-for-4 and not do anything spectacular on his day. So, I thought it was cool that he had talked about it and then hit a home run on the day he tied it and the day he broke it.

Cal is often humbled and embarrassed when compared with Hall of Fame first baseman Lou Gehrig. The Iron Horse posted a career batting average of .340, and hit a major-league record 23 grand slams before his chronic illness sapped his strength and forced his retirement in 1939.

"I know that if Lou Gehrig is looking down on tonight's activities, he isn't concerned about someone playing one more consecutive game than he did," Cal said during his speech on The Night. "Instead, he's viewing tonight as just another example of what is good and right about the great American game."

This might sound funny, but the night that he broke the record, and the days leading up to it, I kind of wanted to watch it as an outsider. I know I'm one of his best friends, but I didn't want to be near him when he was getting all this attention. I just wanted to watch it from a distance. If you look at any pictures from that night, I'm not really close to him. I just wanted to check it all out.

Usually when I go out to left field, I might stop and talk with him for a minute. But, that week when he was getting all those ovations in the fifth inning, I totally avoided him. I just wanted to watch. Knowing what he has gone through and the dedication it took, it was cool to see one of your best friends receive all this positive attention.

The lap was awesome, but you might not believe this: I was trying not to lose my concentration of the game. When the lap was over, I had to hit. It didn't do any good — I struck out.

It's funny, we talked about that day back in 1988 when I first met him. I never really thought for a minute, back in '88, that it would actually happen. I talked with him about it a lot. He asked me why I thought it was important. I told him I had grown up knowing about Lou Gehrig, who almost had 500 homers, and 3,000 hits, and things like that. It will always solidify his place as a baseball legend.

But, to me, it isn't so much the night he broke the record that I remember, or the week building up to it. It wasn't a one-day event. It was like watching his life's work in a way.

People don't understand there are two things going on with The Streak.

One is the unbelievable desire to play and the mental toughness. There may have been guys who have been physically able to put together streaks of 1,000 games, but for one reason or another, they needed a day off. I don't think physically he gets worn down like a normal player, and mentally, he doesn't get worn down like a normal player.

And the thing I think is overlooked when he struggles is: Do you know what an unbelievable asset it is for a team to have its everyday shortstop and a 3-4-5 hitter in the lineup every day? Just think of all the teams that have to go 20, 30 games without their shortstop, which is one of the most critical defensive positions in the field, and offensively, the 3-4-5 hitter, which is the heart of the lineup.

The Streak doesn't mean the same things to me as it does to Cal.

He thinks he can help the team more by being on the field than by taking a day off. I think that's why he was able to do it, because he didn't set out to break the record. He's said to me on numerous occasions, "Yeah, maybe I will be able to help my batting average if I take a few days off, but it wouldn't be the days of rest that would help me . . .

it would be because I'd take the days off that other guys take, against (Roger) Clemens and (Randy) Johnson. It would save myself 25, 30 at-bats facing Cy Young candidates. But, I figure those are the games my team needs me the most."

After the '90 season I saw a change in his outlook and approach to things. I think the one thing we all do as athletes in our own particular sports — because we care about them so much — is we don't get the fun or enjoyment out of them that we should.

I think he saw he needed to have more fun with things and take some of the stress and pressures off him. He probably realized, "Hey this is a cool thing I'm doing. I should be proud of this and get some enjoyment out of it. It shouldn't be a bur-

Wishing he were a fan for a day, lead-off hitter Anderson admitted getting caught up in the hoopla surrounding The Night. But Brady remained focused enough to record a hit in the Orioles' 4-2 victory over the Angels.

The Orioles' games of Sept. 5 and 6 were played with baseballs sporting a specially designed "Streak Week" logo.

President Bill Clinton and a capacity crowd of 46,272 celebrated every pitch of Cal's streak-breaking performance, which included a home run and yet another flawless effort in the field.

den. Breaking one of the most prestigious records in all of sports, I should be getting fun out of this."

I don't think The Streak has obscured his other accomplishments. I think they go hand-in-hand. He's a two-time MVP, and to me, the best shortstop who ever played. Cal is probably the most famous baseball player in the world. He's a playing, living legend, so it's hard to say The Streak has obscured anything.

His demeanor, his character, the way he conducts himself, the time he spends signing auto-graphs. All these things combine to make people root for him and root for The Streak. That's what everybody rooted for that day. A lot of times when people break records it's not that way. A lot of people didn't want Hank Aaron to break Babe Ruth's record, as ridiculous as that sounds now. But, I don't think anybody wanted something to happen to Cal so he couldn't break Lou Gehrig's record.

During the days leading up to Sept. 6, 1995, the night Cal Ripken broke Lou Gehrig's consecutive games record at 2,131, the Baltimore Orioles counted down the games by dropping a banner from the facade of the Warehouse overlooking right field at Camden Yards.

At this time, the video board would play highlights of Ripken's career and the crowd would rise for another standing ovation. This was a perfect time, along with pitching changes, for Orioles outfielder Brady Anderson, one of Ripken's closest friends, to practice the speech he would give before a packed house and a national television audience.

Here's part of what Anderson said that night:

"For 14 years, Cal Ripken has played for the Orioles with skill, determination and dedication. His inspiration has always been a love for the game, his teammates and the devoted fans of Baltimore.

"I know Cal is honored to be in the company of such a legend [as Lou Gehrig]. Just as we know that each man's accomplishments and contributions enhance, rather than diminish, the others.

"Cal, you have inspired many teammates; you have delighted millions of fans; you have given the nation uncountable memories. Your pride in, and love for, the game are at a level few others will reach.

"This day marks a historic occasion in baseball, and we warmly congratulate you on this achievement. But Cal, please . . . this week has been fun, but also a bit hectic. Promise us that this will happen once every 2,131 games."

John Delcos covers the Orioles for The York (Penn.) Daily Record.

Anderson thinks The Streak is only part of what makes Cal "the best shortstop who ever played" and a "living legend," and believes his two AL MVP awards, his home run record for shortstops and his multiple fielding records will not be forgotten.